GET INTO
ART
ANIMALS

SUSIE BROOKS

MAC ‌‌ OOKS
993738205 X

First published 2013 by Kingfisher
an imprint of Macmillan Children's Books

This edition published 2014 by Macmillan Children's Books
a division of Macmillan Publishers Limited
20 New Wharf Road, London N1 9RR
Basingstoke and Oxford
Associated companies throughout the world
www.panmacmillan.com

Edited by Catherine Brereton
Designed by Jane Tassie
Project photography by Geoff Dann

ISBN 978-1-4472-6393-7

Picture credits
The Publisher would like to thank the following for permission to reproduce their material.
Every care has been taken to trace copyright holders. However, if there have been
unintentional omissions or failure to trace copyright holders, we apologize and will,
if informed, endeavour to make corrections in any future edition.
Top = t; Bottom = b; Centre = c; Left = l; Right = r
Cover and page 26 *Portrait of Maurice* by Andy Warhol/The National Galleries of Scotland,
Edinburgh; page 6 *The Snail* by Henri Matisse/The Tate Gallery, London; 8 *Suspense* by Edwin
Landseer/V & A Museum, London/Bridgeman Art Gallery; 10 *Crinkly Giraffe* by Alexander
Calder/The Calder Foundation/Private Collection/Bridgeman Art Library; 12 *The Bird* by
Georges Braque/Private Collection/Bridgeman Art Library; 14 *Peacock and Magpie* by Edward
Bawden/with the kind permission of Peyton Skipwith/Fry Art Gallery, Saffron Walden/
Bridgeman Art Gallery; 16 *Fish (E59)* by M. C. Escher/The Escher Foundation, The Netherlands;
18 *Carnival of Harlequin* by Joan Miró/Albright-Knox Art Gallery, Buffalo/The Art Archive; 20
Shutterstock/Terry Alexander; 21 Shutterstock/2009fotofriends; 22 *Yellow Cow* by Franz Marc/
Solomon R. Guggenheim Museum, New York/AKG London; 24 Bridgeman Art Library/Paul
Freeman; 28 *Jockeys in the Rain* by Edgar Degas/CSG CIC Glasgow Museums Collection.

CONTENTS

PICTURE AN ANIMAL

If you were going to draw an animal, what would it be?
You have so much choice, it might be hard to decide! Animals are
a great subject for artists because there are so many shapes, colours
and characters to choose from. Friendly pets, fierce wild beasts,
bright birds and even imaginary creatures have made their
way into paintings, sculptures and other works of art.

Look at the different ways in which **animals have inspired
famous artists** – then **let them inspire you too!** Each page
of this book will tell you about a work of art and the person who
created it. When you lift the flap, you'll find a project based
on the artwork. Don't feel you have to copy it exactly.
Half the fun of art is making something your own!

GETTING STARTED

There's a checklist on page 31 that will tell you
what you need for each project, but it's a good idea
to read through the steps before you begin. There
are also some handy tips on the next page…

Always have a **pencil** and
rubber handy. Making a
rough **sketch** can help you
plan a project and see how
it's going to look.

PICK YOUR PAINT...

Acrylic paints are thick and bright – they're great for strong colours, or textures like shaggy fur. **Ready-mix paints** are cheaper than acrylics but still bright. Use them when you need lots of paint.

Watercolours give a thinner colouring – try them over oil pastel or crayon, or draw on them in ink.

Use a mixture of thick and thin **paintbrushes**. Have a jam jar or plastic cup of water ready to rinse them in and a **palette** or paper plate for mixing paint.

TRY PASTELS...

Oil pastels have a bright, waxy look, like crayons. **Soft pastels** can be smudged and blended like chalk.

acrylic paint

Lay some newspaper on your surface before you start to paint!

watercolour paint

sponged paint

oil pastels

soft pastel

For painting, use thick **cartridge** or **watercolour paper** – anything too thin will wrinkle. **Pastel paper** has a rough surface that holds onto the colour.

Collect a range of **coloured papers and card** for collage and 3-D models.

Ready to start?
Let's **get into art!**

Look around the home for other art materials. Useful things include sponges, rags or cloths, cocktail sticks, drinking straws, scissors, glue, string, roller brushes and a hole punch.

In real life this picture is enormous – nearly 3 metres square! It's a collage of painted paper stuck onto white paper and then onto canvas. Matisse called this method 'drawing with scissors'.

H. Matisse 53

SNIP A SNAKE

Matisse loved finding patterns in nature. Look at some pictures of snakes to see how they bend and curl, then try making this snaky collage.

Your card can be huge, like Matisse's, or small if you have less space.

straight edge here

1 Take a white sheet of card as your base. Cut out some strips of coloured paper – use the edges of the paper so they're straight along one side. Lay them around your card to make a border. Glue them down.

2 To make your snake, cut out simple block shapes from different coloured papers.

Let some pieces overlap the border.

3 Lay the shapes in a twisting pattern, thinking about which colours you are placing next to each other.

4 Move the shapes around until you're happy with your snake, then glue them down.

Use a big piece for the head. If you like, you can add a forked tongue!

THE SNAIL

Henri Matisse 1953

You might have to look twice before spotting the snail in this picture! There's no outline, but Henri Matisse has created the idea of a snail by arranging coloured shapes in a spiral pattern.

Drawing with colour

When Matisse made *The Snail*, he was 84 years old. He wasn't well enough to stand and draw, so instead he used colour as his starting point. His assistants painted sheets of paper in plain colours, then Matisse cut or tore them into shapes.

Matisse chose his colours carefully. They are not the colours of a real snail, but they are warm and bright. Matisse knew that complementary colours, such as red and green, look stronger when they're put next to each other. The way he has placed the pieces makes them zing out, as if the snail is moving. It seems to be wriggling out of the jagged orange frame!

WHO WAS MATISSE?

Henri Matisse was born in France in 1869. His first job was as a lawyer, but he didn't like it much. At the age of 20, he became ill and had to spend long hours in bed. His mother gave him a paint box to pass the time, and straight away he knew he would become an artist! Matisse made many famous paintings in his distinctive colourful style.

FURRY FRIENDS

Landseer's work was very detailed, but **you can paint furry animals in different ways.** Try these!

Use the brush tip for the tail, legs and ears.

1 Use a square-ended brush to paint the basic shape – it could be a dog like this, or your pet or other favourite animal.

2 With a clean brush, add downward streaks in a lighter colour.

Vary the length of the streaks.

3 Now paint white highlights using short flicks of a fine brush. Use dark paint for the eye, nose and mouth, and a few shadowy streaks under the belly.

Here are some other ways of **painting fur**.

Scratch into thick wet paint with a cocktail stick.

Dab dark then light paint with a piece of sponge.

SUSPENSE

Sir Edwin Landseer 1861

Who is this dog waiting for? What's behind the door?

Landseer wanted us to ask questions like this when he painted *Suspense*! His picture tells a story, but he leaves us to work out what it is.

See the story

If you look closely, you'll spot some clues. There are drops of blood on the floor… a feather torn from a hat… a knight's armoured gloves on the table. It seems that the dog's master has been wounded and carried through the house.

The dog sits on his haunches, staring closely at the door. We can tell that he is worried and longs to rush to his master's side. Landseer's skilful brushwork makes us feel that the animal is alive. The light glints on his anxious face and hairs stand up on his neck. He leans forward, ready to spring up at any moment – but we can only imagine what he'll find.

WHO WAS LANDSEER?

Edwin Landseer was born into a family of artists in England in 1802. He began to draw as soon as he could hold a pencil, and was exhibiting work by the age of 13. Animals were his favourite subjects – he even had a breed of dog named after him! Landseer made sculptures too, including the huge bronze lions in London's Trafalgar Square.

CRINKLY MONKEYS

Calder turned flat materials into 3-D objects. Try it yourself with these crinkly monkeys!

Stick the head on here.

In 1926, Calder made a whole circus of animals and actors out of wood, wire, cork and cloth. He kept them in suitcases and travelled around giving performances!

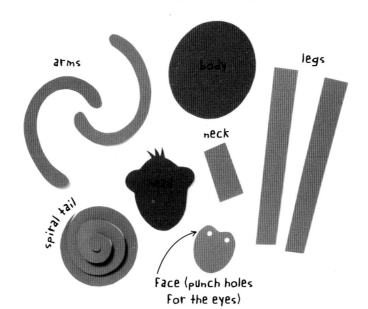

arms

body

legs

neck

spiral tail

head

Face (punch holes for the eyes)

1 Cut out shapes like these from coloured card.

3 Glue one end of the neck to the body, then stick on the head. Next glue on the arms, then the legs and tail.

legs

spiral tail

neck

2 Fold the leg and neck strips back and forth to make them crinkly. Gently stretch out the tail. Glue the face onto the head.

4 Dangle your monkey from a hook, shelf or doorknob. Then make some monkey friends!

Try hanging one monkey from another!

CRINKLY GIRAFFE

Alexander Calder 1971

This giraffe isn't going anywhere – but if you walk around it, it almost seems to move. Calder was famous for his dynamic sculptures, some of which really do move.

Animobiles

Crinkly Giraffe is made of painted metal, cut into simple shapes. The flat metal looks different from different angles, so the crinkly neck seems to shift and turn. Calder made a whole series of crinkly animals like this. His wife named them Animobiles!

The word Animobile comes from animal and mobile – and Calder invented the mobile too. His first one had a motor, but he soon realized that hanging shapes would move on their own. He experimented with different materials, including metal, wire and wood. Little did he know how popular his invention would become!

WHO WAS CALDER?

Alexander Calder was born in 1898 in the USA. His father was a sculptor and his mother a painter, but Alexander studied to be an engineer. Later, he went to art school and travelled to Paris to work. He used nature as his inspiration for abstract mobiles, standing 'stabiles' and giant outdoor sculptures that are displayed around the world.

Use simple shapes like Braque's to make a

SEASIDE STRING PRINT

1 First draw your seaside shapes onto thick cardboard.

Choose one main animal and some smaller shapes.

2 Taking one shape at a time, cover the outline with strong craft glue. Stick a piece of thick string or cord all around it.

Try gluing on some other materials. They need to be as thick as the string.

cut-up bits of spongy kitchen cloth

drinking straws

bubble wrap

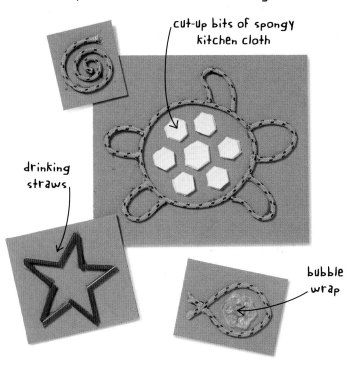

3 When the glue is dry, use a roller or sponge to spread paint over the design. Turn it over onto a piece of white paper. Press firmly, then gently lift it off.

The print will be in reverse.

If you don't get a good print the first time, try again!

4 Cut out your best prints and glue them onto coloured paper.

Dip the end of a straw or pencil in white paint to print some bubbles!

THE BIRD

Georges Braque 1949

On first glance, you might think a child made this picture! The shapes are simple and the colours are bright. In fact Braque created it for children, as part of a project for schools after the Second World War.

Primary print

The idea came from a lady in London, who decided that schools should have great pieces of art on their walls. She travelled to Paris and persuaded artists such as Braque to help. They produced work using a new type of lithograph printing. Each print had a border around the edge, so there wasn't any need for a frame!

Braque was fond of bold, simple shapes – and he particularly loved painting birds. In this print the shapes are familiar, but they float in an imaginary scene. The primary colours red, yellow and blue look cheerful and fresh against the white.

WHO WAS BRAQUE?

Georges Braque was born in France in 1882. He trained as a painter and decorator, but studied art in the evenings and soon took up Fauvism – a new style of painting in bright colours. He then turned to Cubism, using simple shapes and collage. During the First World War, he was injured and had to stop painting. Later he experimented with prints and sculpture.

With the kind permission of Peyton Skipwith/Fry Art Gallery, Saffron Walden/Bridgeman Art Gallery

Try scraping into paint to create some

FABULOUS FEATHERS

1 Draw the outline of a peacock on a piece of thick paper or card. Start with the body then add a big, fan-like tail.

Draw circular markings on the tail.

2 Colour your peacock with a thick layer of oil pastel. Use light, bright colours like these.

4 While the paint is still wet, scrape feathery patterns into it. If you make a mistake, just paint over it and scrape again!

The oil pastel colours show through.

3 Now squeeze some dark blue and dark green acrylic paint onto a palette. Paint over the oil pastel – try to work quickly and lay the paint on thickly.

Paint the green tail, then the blue spots and body.

You could use the end of a paintbrush...

a cocktail stick...

or the end of a teaspoon.

PEACOCK AND MAGPIE

Edward Bawden 1970

What's the first thing you notice in this picture? Probably the peacock with its dazzling, fanned-out tail! Bawden shows us the proud character of the bird as he illustrates one of Aesop's Fables.

A telling tail

Fables are stories with a moral, which means they have a lesson to teach us. In this one, the peacock declares he should be king of the birds. The others are impressed by his grand appearance, but the magpie questions whether he could protect the birds against eagles and other hunters. The moral is: listen to the advice of others.

Bawden cut this scene into lino then printed it in ink on paper. The crisp lines make the story clear, but they are decorative too. The yellow of the peacock catches our eye, just as it attracts the birds. Only when we look more closely do we see the magpie talking wisely to the crowd.

WHO WAS BAWDEN?

Edward Bawden was born in England in 1903. He became famous for many types of art, including book illustrations, advertising posters, murals and metalwork furniture. He made tile paintings for the London Underground and even designed china for passenger ships!

Escher made 137 drawings like this one. He tessellated lizards, frogs, insects, birds and even human shapes. His work has always fascinated mathematicians – but surprisingly, Escher struggled with maths at school!

Make this simple template for an Escher-style
FISH SQUISH

1 Glue a piece of squared paper to some card and cut out a 5cm x 5cm square. Mark two triangles across opposite corners, as shown.

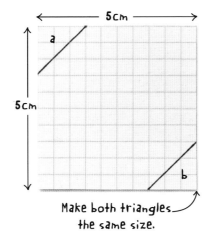

5cm

5cm

a

b

Make both triangles the same size.

2 Cut off one triangle and carefully tape it to the other side of the square, like this.

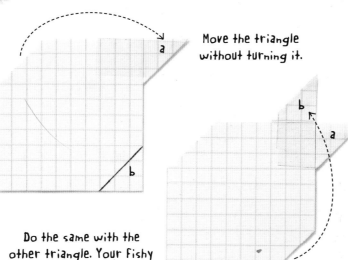

Move the triangle without turning it.

a

b

b

a

Do the same with the other triangle. Your fishy template is complete!

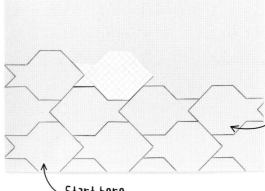

When you get to the end of a row, turn the template over and go back the other way.

Start here.

3 At the bottom of a large sheet of paper, draw around your template in pencil. Then move it along so the tail slots into the head and draw around it again. Keep going like this!

These fish were outlined in marker pen, shaded with oil pastel then washed over with watercolour paint.

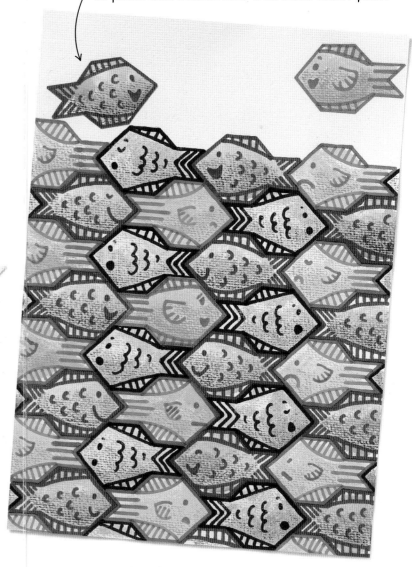

4 When you've got a full page of fish, colour them in!

FISH (E59)

M. C. Escher 1942

No matter how hard you look, you won't find a gap between these fish! Escher has taken the shape of an animal and turned it into a perfect pattern. It's called a tessellation.

Tile style

Tessellation is basically tiling – every shape fits together edge to edge. Of course it's much harder to tile an animal shape than a simple square or triangle! Escher used geometric shapes as his starting point, then changed them into curving forms. He twisted, flipped and repeated them to make patterns.

We can see two types of fish in this picture. It's like looking through a kaleidoscope. Escher drew them on graph paper, then coloured them with pencils, ink and watercolour. He liked the idea that the pattern could go on forever, though he had to stop when he got near the edge of the page!

WHO WAS ESCHER?

Maurits Cornelis Escher was born in Holland in 1898. His interest in linking shapes began on a trip to the Alhambra, a Moorish castle in Spain. He drew and sketched on his travels and went home to make prints of the buildings he'd seen. In his work he loved to trick the eye and play with impossible spaces. He turned the world into a puzzling and unbelievable place!

Let your imagination go wild with these
CRAZY CREATURES

You can paint straight over fiddly lines like this one — the waxy crayon will show through.

1 On a piece of thick white paper, draw some shapes in black wax crayon. Don't think about it too much – just draw!

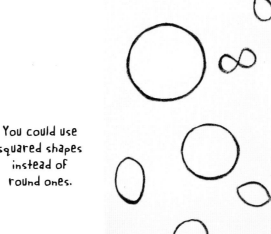

You could use squared shapes instead of round ones.

3 Colour in your picture with water-based paint.

Miró made sculptures too. Try creating some **mad monsters** out of modelling clay!

2 Now start adding lines, swirls and other shapes. Turn your page into a circus of crazy creatures!

Let some lines go right to the edge of the page.

CARNIVAL OF HARLEQUIN

Joan Miró 1924–25

Have you ever seen things in a dream that wouldn't make sense in real life? Miró takes us to a dream-like place in this painting of a strange but lively party!

Carnival chaos

The creatures here aren't animals as we know them, but you can probably recognize some shapes. There are winged insects, spidery forms, a fish and two cats playing with string. Bright characters leap across the canvas, dancing to musical notes that are floating in the air.

When Miró painted this, he was poor and hungry. Perhaps that's why the main figure, the Harlequin, has a hole in his guitar-shaped stomach. He looks sad and still in this happy, playful scene. Miró said that hunger made him hallucinate, or see things that weren't really there.

WHO WAS MIRÓ?

Joan Miró was born in Spain in 1893. On a trip to Paris in the 1920s, he became interested in an art style called Surrealism. He was fascinated by the imagination, particularly children's make-believe, and grew famous for his colourful paintings and sculptures that seem to come from an imaginary world.

CRAFTY TOTEM

Make your own totem pole out of a card tube and paper!

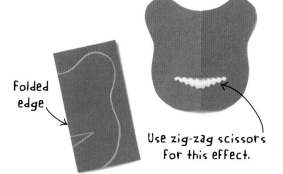

The Thunderbird brings thunder with his flapping wings and lightning with a flash of his eyes! Below him is Sea-bear and a killer whale, then a man with a frog. Lower down we see the yellow-nosed Bakwas – 'wild man of the woods' – and Dzunukwa, a child-eating giantess. They are all characters from Kwakwaka'wakw legend.

height of tube →

Tape the strips at the back.

1 Cut some paper so it's the right size to wrap around your tube. You could tape several strips together, like this.

Folded edge

Use zig-zag scissors for this effect.

2 Cut out some simple animal shapes. To make them symmetrical, cut them from a folded piece of paper.

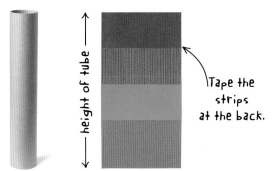

Add feathers, paws and other shapes to the sides.

3 Glue your animals down the centre of the paper. The more shapes you cut and layer, the more decorative the pole will look.

Cut slits in the tube to slot the wings in.

4 Wrap your finished design around the tube and tape it at the back. For a final touch, you could make some colourful card wings.

TOTEM POLES

Wayne Alfred and Beau Dick 1991
and Ellen Neel 1955 (near left)

It's hard to imagine that these colourful carvings began life as whole cedar trees! Totem poles show the skill of traditional artists from the north-west coast of North America.

Tall stories

It can take a year to carve a totem pole! The idea is to tell a story, perhaps about an event, a legend or people in a particular family. Each pole is a stack of characters that have special meaning in the local culture. Many animals and birds are believed to have special powers or bring different kinds of luck.

The green-faced figure on the far left is Red Cedar-Bark Man. In traditional tales, he survived a great flood and gave people the first canoe. You can see him holding a patterned boat, with the legendary Quolus bird spreading its wings above him. Quolus is the younger brother of Thunderbird, who tops the pole on the near left.

TOTEM TRADITION

Native Americans have carved totem poles for hundreds of years, but because wood rots the oldest examples have not survived. These two were made by modern-day artists from the Kwakwaka'wakw tribe of British Columbia, Canada. You can tell they are modern because of the bright paint colours.

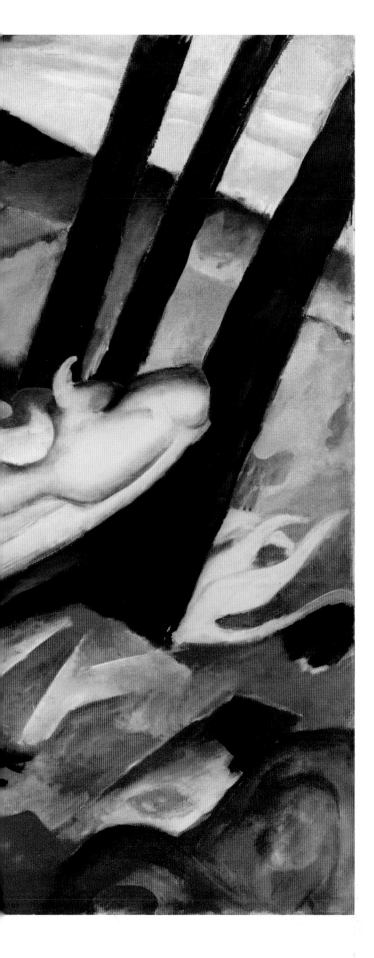

How do colours make you feel? Find out with these

MOODY SHEEP

Yellow makes a lively, happy sheep.

1 Pick a paint colour and squeeze some onto a palette or paper plate. Dip a sponge in the paint, and use it to paint a fluffy sheep's body.

2 Look at the colour and decide how it makes you feel. Think of that mood as you paint in the sheep's head and legs.

Lilac is calm for a snoozy sheep.

This green is gloomy for a grumpy sheep.

3 Repeat steps 1 and 2 using different colours.

What colours would you use for an **angry sheep**, a **lazy sheep** or a **startled** one?

4 Why not make a big picture with all your moody sheep? Take a large piece of paper and sponge-paint a colourful background. Cut out your sheep and glue them on!

YELLOW COW

Franz Marc 1911

Have you ever seen a yellow cow with blue spots? Probably not! Franz Marc loved to paint from nature, but he didn't copy exactly what he saw.

Inside out

Marc said that he wanted to recreate animals 'from the inside'. He used colours to express different feelings. For him, yellow was cheerful, gentle and female – like this cow, leaping happily across a sunny scene.

Marc's style of painting is known as Expressionism. It captures a mood, rather than a realistic view of the world, and makes us look at things in a different way. In fact, Marc knew very well how to paint a realistic cow. He spent long hours sketching and studying animals, and even taught other artists about their shape and form.

WHO WAS MARC?

Franz Marc was born in Germany in 1880, the son of a landscape painter. He took up art at the age of 20 and was soon organizing exhibitions with other Expressionist artists. Marc was fascinated by animals. He wanted to paint the world through their eyes. Sadly, he died young, fighting in the First World War.

Transform a paper plate with your own

DISHY DRAGON

When this dish was made, artists didn't have paints like ours. Instead they used pigments – solid cakes of colour that they ground into powder and mixed with liquid. This blue comes from a substance called cobalt. It has been used in Chinese pottery for more than 1,000 years.

1 Sketch your dragon in pencil first. Draw the head then a long, snake-like body and tail. Add four legs with clawed feet.

2 Use a fine brush and thick paint to cover the outline in blue. Then colour it in with a wide brush and watery paint.

You can layer more colour to make some areas darker.

3 Experiment with different brushmarks before adding detail to your dragon.

Use the tip of a fine brush for delicate lines.

A flick of a brush gives scaly shapes like this.

Try a sideways dab of the brush...

and long, sideways strokes.

4 Decorate your dragon with scales and fins. Add swirling patterns around it.

You could add a thin coat of glitter paint to make your dragon gleam!

DRAGON DISH

Chinese artist 1600–35

A snake's body, an eagle's claws, the scales of a fish... you can see several animals in a Chinese dragon!
These ones are painted on a porcelain dish, surrounded by decorative swirls.

Curious creatures

Artists can have fun with dragons because they're imaginary – no one really knows what they look like! In Chinese mythology they are often friendly, unlike the fire-breathing dragons of Europe. They are rulers of water and the weather, and symbols of power and good luck.

These three dragons have lizard-like head frills and wriggling bodies that twist around the dish. Their four claws show that they are ordinary dragons – five claws would mean they belonged to an emperor. The round shapes the dragons are chasing are magical flaming pearls. Everything is painted in a single colour – cobalt blue. The artist used a fine brush for the detail, then filled in the outlines. In some parts the colour is layered to give a darker effect.

HOW WAS IT MADE?

This type of ceramic painting is called 'underglaze blue'. The blue design is painted onto dried white porcelain, then coated with a clear protective glaze. Afterwards it is baked, or fired, at a high temperature. This hardens the porcelain and sets the glaze.

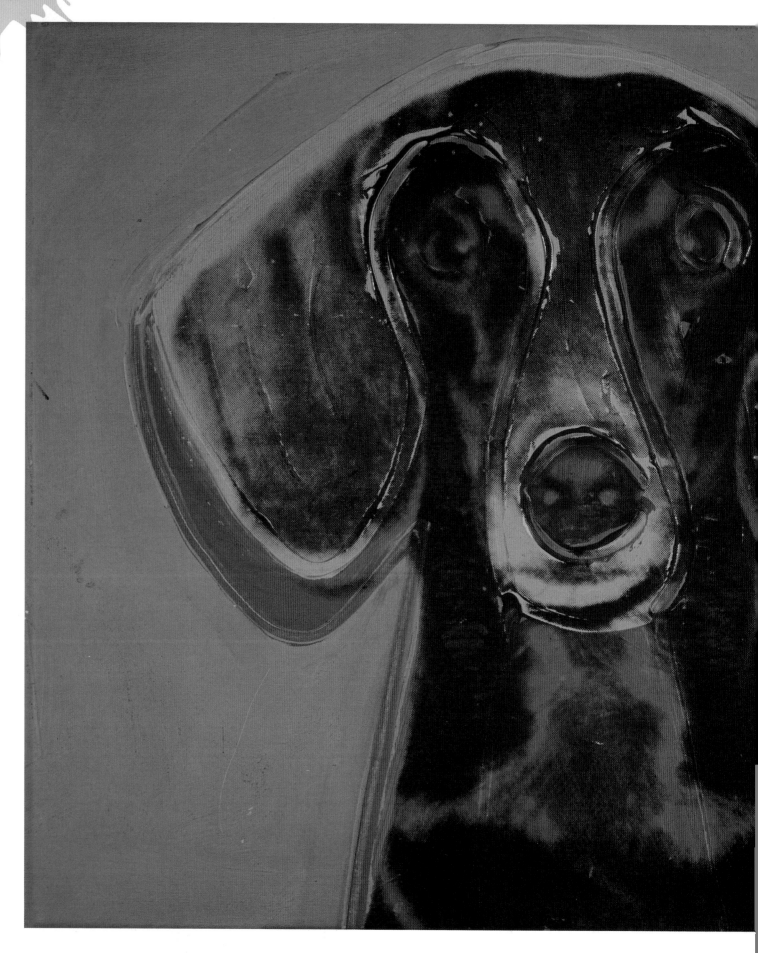

COLOURFUL CATS

Warhol's silkscreen method was complicated, but **you can get a similar effect with a simple stencil.**

1 On a piece of card, draw the outline of an animal and carefully cut it out. You'll end up with two stencils like these.

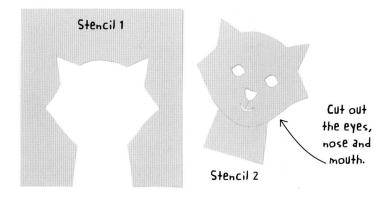

Stencil 1

Stencil 2

Cut out the eyes, nose and mouth.

2 Lay Stencil 1 on a piece of thick paper and fix it with paper clips. Sponge yellow paint all over it.

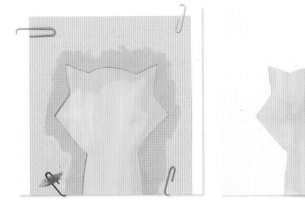

3 When the paint is dry, lift the stencil and move it slightly down and to one side. Sponge red paint unevenly over it, then leave to dry.

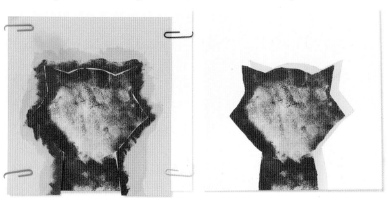

4 Now lay Stencil 2 on top of the picture and sponge blue paint over the holes. Leave to dry, then remove the stencil. Cut out the animal and stick it onto a coloured background.

You can print whiskers by dipping the edge of a strip of card in paint.

Warhol often repeated his prints in different colours. **Try making a set like this!**

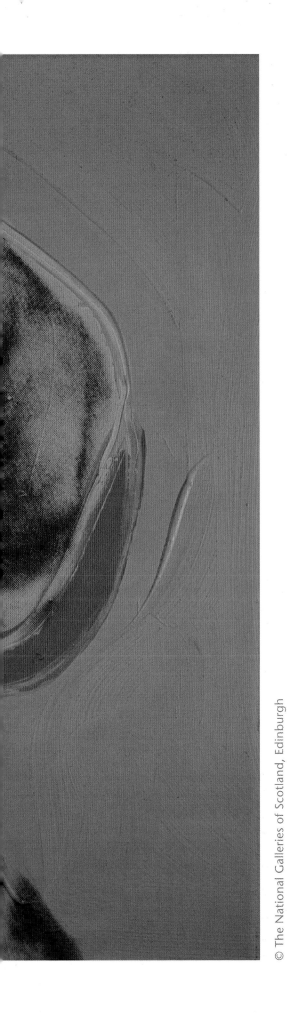

PORTRAIT OF MAURICE

Andy Warhol 1976

Andy Warhol was known for his pictures of rich and famous people – but he happily made portraits of their pets too! This dachshund belonged to the art collector Gabrielle Keiller.

Dazzling dog

Maurice the dachshund wasn't actually blue, pink and red! Warhol liked experimenting with bold, attention-grabbing colours – they reminded him of adverts and modern life. He took photographs of Maurice, then worked on them back in his studio. To make this screen print, he pushed ink through a type of stencil on a silk screen.

Warhol once wrote, 'I never met a pet I didn't like' – and in fact he had two dachshunds of his own. You can see his love of animals in this portrait of Maurice, who looks straight at us with appealing eyes.

WHO WAS WARHOL?

Andy Warhol was born in the USA in 1928. His talent for art showed from a young age, and he loved films, photography and cartoons. He became famous for his Pop Art, inspired by advertising images and glamorous stars. Archie, one of his dachshunds, was often photographed by his side!

RAINY RACEHORSE

Degas learned to draw by copying.

Practise sketching from pictures of horses. Then have a go at this pastel drawing on blue textured paper.

1 First draw the outline in pencil. If you want to copy this horse, follow the shapes in the order below. Draw it to one side of the page, like Degas did.

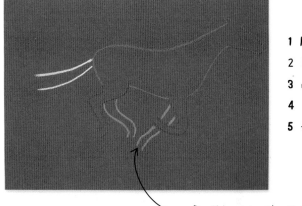

1 head
2 body
3 near legs
4 far legs
5 tail

Don't worry about the feet!

2 Use a chalk pastel to colour your horse. Smudge with your finger to spread the colour.

Smudge the pastel at the horse's feet.

3 Choose a darker pastel to draw shadows on the underside of the horse. Add highlights to the upper areas with a lighter colour.

Draw an eye and a flowing mane.

You can blend two colours by smudging them gently.

Let some rain go over the horse.

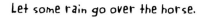

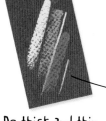

Do thick and thin streaks of rain.

Make diagonal flicks near the horse's feet.

4 Use marks like these to draw some green grass, then a rainy blue-grey sky.

Make downward streaks with the tip of a pastel.

JOCKEYS IN THE RAIN

Edgar Degas *about* 1883–86

Looking at this picture, we know just how the horses are feeling!

Degas shows us their nerves and excitement before a race, with the added restlessness of a storm.

Stormy start

Strong, colourful marks bring this pastel scene to life. Degas has drawn long streaks of blue to show the thrashing fall of rain. His diagonal strokes of green make the grass seem to sway, and the distant trees lean in the wind.

Notice how the horses are kept to one side of the drawing – some are even cut off at the picture's edge. Degas wanted us to feel the tension as the horses wait in line. Their poses are full of movement, as if they're ready to charge ahead over the open ground.

WHO WAS DEGAS?

Edgar Degas was born in France in 1834. By the age of 18, he had created his own art studio. He loved to make pictures of everyday scenes, and was fascinated by dancers and horses and how they moved. The way he cropped his figures and showed them from odd angles was seen as very daring at the time.

ART WORDS AND INFO

abstract Not representing an actual object, place or living thing. Abstract art often focuses on simplified shapes, lines, colours or use of space.

carving An artwork made by cutting into a solid material, such as wood or stone.

collage A picture made by sticking bits of paper, fabric or other objects onto a surface.

complementary colours Colours that are opposite each other on the colour wheel (see panel below). If you place complementary colours next to each other, they look brighter.

Cubism (1907–1920s) An art style that involved making images using simple geometric shapes.

exhibit To display work for people to see, for example in a gallery or museum.

Expressionist From the art style Expressionism (1905–1920s). Expressionist art was about feelings and emotions, often shown through distorted shapes or colours.

Fauvism (about 1905–1910) An art style that focussed on strong, vibrant colours and bold brushstrokes.

illustration A picture that explains or decorates a story or other text.

lino A tough, washable material with a smooth surface. Artists can scrape a design into it, then cover it with paint or ink to make a print.

lithograph A type of print, where the design is drawn onto stone or metal with a greasy substance. This is then covered with ink, which clings only to the greasy areas, and printed onto paper.

mural A picture painted straight onto a wall.

COLOUR CONNECTIONS

In art there are three primary colours – **red**, **yellow** and **blue**. These are colours that can't be mixed from any others. Each primary colour has has an opposite, or complementary, which is made by mixing the other two.

If you mix a colour with its complementary, you'll get a shade of brown.

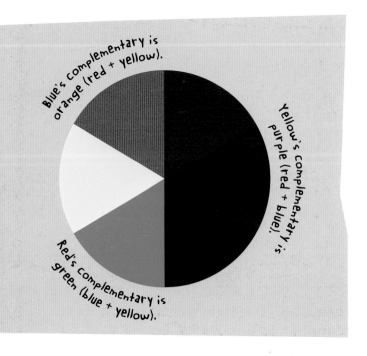

Blue's complementary is orange (red + yellow).

Yellow's complementary is purple (red + blue).

Red's complementary is green (blue + yellow).

Pop Art (mid 1950s–1960s) An art style that celebrated the bold, bright images of advertising, cartoon strips and modern life.

porcelain A white, clay-based material that is used to make china (or ceramics).

print A way of transferring an image from one surface to another. Prints are often made by spreading ink over a raised or engraved design, then pressing it onto paper. This makes a reverse or negative image that can be reproduced many times.

screen print A print made by dragging ink over a stencil marked onto a silk screen. The ink goes through tiny holes in the silk that aren't covered by the stencil.

sculpt To make three-dimensional art, called sculpture. Carving and clay modelling are both types of sculpture. Someone who does this is called a sculptor.

sketch A rough drawing or painting, often made to help plan a final artwork.

stencil A template that allows paint or ink to go through the holes but blocks out other areas.

studio A place where an artist or photographer works.

Surrealism (1924–1940s) An art style that explored the world of dreams, the imagination and the 'non-thinking' mind. Surrealist works often show familiar things, but in unexpected or impossible ways.

symmetrical When one side of a shape is the mirror image of the other side.

texture The feel of a surface, such as rough fur or smooth scales.

PROJECT CHECKLIST

These are the materials you'll need for each project. The ones in brackets are useful but you can manage without!

Snip a snake (page 7): white card, brightly coloured papers, scissors, glue

Furry friends (page 9): acrylic paints, paintbrushes, sponge, cocktail stick

Crinkly monkeys (page 11): coloured card, scissors, hole punch, glue

Seaside string print (page 13): stiff cardboard, pencil, craft glue, thick string or cord, scissors, sponge or roller, thick paint, white paper, coloured paper, (bubble wrap, spongy kitchen cloth, drinking straws)

Fabulous feathers (page 15): thick white paper or card, pencil, oil pastels, acrylic paints, paintbrushes, (cocktail stick, teaspoon)

Fish squish (page 17): squared paper, thin card, glue, ruler, pencil, scissors, sticky tape, white paper, colouring materials (eg marker pens, oil pastels, watercolour paint, paintbrushes)

Crazy creatures (page 19): thick white paper, black wax crayon, water-based paints, paintbrushes, (modelling clay)

Crafty totem (page 21): card tube, different coloured papers, ruler, sticky tape, pencil or chalk, scissors, (zig-zag scissors), glue, stiff card

Moody sheep (page 23): thick white paper, sponge, bright paints, palette or paper plate, large piece of paper, paintbrush, scissors, glue

Dishy dragon (page 25): paper plate, pencil, blue paint, fine paintbrush, wide paintbrush, (glitter or glitter paint)

Colourful cats (page 27): thin card, pencil, scissors, thick white paper, paper clips, bright paints, sponge, coloured card, glue, strip of card

Rainy racehorse (page 29): pencil, blue pastel paper, soft pastels or chalks

INDEX